POLAR BEARS

by Michèle Dufresne

Pioneer Valley Educational Press, Inc.

TABLE OF CONTENTS

About Polar Bears 4

Habitat and Diet...8

Hunters of the Arctic 14

Threatened Species.......................................18

Polar Bear Cubs...20

Glossary 24

Index..24

ABOUT POLAR BEARS

Polar bears are very large bears. They live and hunt on the ice and in the extremely cold waters of the Arctic Ocean.

Polar bears have bodies built for cold temperatures and for moving across snow, ice, and open water. They are excellent swimmers. Polar bears can swim long distances and are able to stay under water for as long as 2 minutes.

Polar bears are the biggest **carnivores** living on land. Adult male polar bears can weigh up to 1,500 pounds.

Polar bears have two layers of fur to keep them warm. Their fur looks white or tan, but the hair is actually hollow and transparent. Their coat provides camouflage, making it hard for their prey to see them coming.

coat

ears

Polar bears have small ears but excellent hearing. They have a strong sense of smell that can detect seals up to 1 mile away.

Polar bears have large feet to help carry their weight on snow and thin ice. The pads of their paws are covered with small, soft bumps, which provide traction on the ice. Polar bears have claws that are deeply scooped on the underside to help dig in the ice.

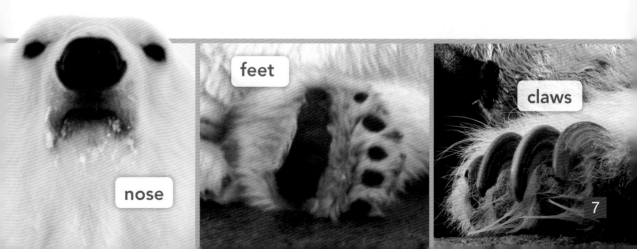

nose

feet

claws

HABITAT AND DIET

Polar bears live in the Arctic.
During the Arctic winter, large areas
of the ocean are covered with ice.

In some places, the ice is broken into floating
pieces called ice floes. Polar bears can swim
for many miles from one ice floe to another.
They have been seen in open Arctic waters
as far as 200 miles from land.

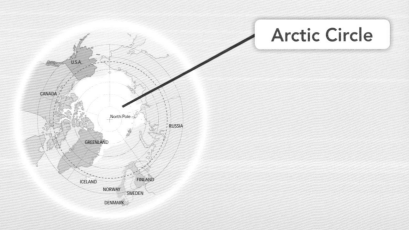

Arctic Circle

In the spring and summer, the ice melts completely in some areas of the Arctic. Then, polar bears must go onto land and wait through the warm months for the next freeze.

Each summer, some polar bears move to the ice farther north where it remains frozen year-round. They follow **migrating** seals to new locations.

If there are no seals to eat,
polar bears will eat other wild animals,
including birds, eggs, rodents, shellfish,
and crabs. They sometimes eat plants,
such as roots and berries.
Polar bears will even eat seaweed.

HUNTERS OF THE ARCTIC

Polar bears are excellent hunters.
Their white coats help them hide from their prey in snow. In the cold Arctic, there are many seals for the polar bears to hunt and eat.

Polar bears wait quietly by holes in the ice where seals come up for air.

When the seal **exhales**, the polar bear reaches into the hole and catches it.

Polar bears also hunt seals
that are resting on the ice.

The polar bear walks closer and closer
toward the resting seal.
Then, the polar bear crouches down and waits.
If the seal does not notice, it creeps closer
on its belly and then suddenly attacks.

Polar bears hunt small whales and walruses, too.

THREATENED SPECIES

Many scientists believe global warming is a threat to polar bears.

Polar bears hunt seals from sea ice. But as temperatures rise in the Arctic, the sea ice melts earlier in the year. This forces polar bears to go to shore where there is less food for them to eat. They also have to swim longer distances because there is less ice to walk on.

Polar bears are also threatened by hunters, pollution, and oil spills.

POLAR BEAR CUBS

Mother polar bears prepare for their new babies by digging dens in the snow.

The mother goes into the den and enters a **dormant** state similar to **hibernation**.

Polar bear cubs are born blind. They are covered with a light, downy fur and weigh fewer than 2 pounds. Most mothers have a litter of two cubs. The family stays in the den for several months.

The cubs grow and grow and can weigh as much as 33 pounds when they are ready to leave the den. For about 2 weeks, the family stays near the den. Then they begin the long walk to the sea ice, where their mother can catch seals once again.

Most cubs are **weaned** at 2 ½ years of age. The mother polar bear chases them away or leaves them. After the mother leaves, the sibling cubs sometimes travel and share food together for weeks or months.

GLOSSARY

carnivores: animals that eat meat

dormant: inactive as if sleeping

exhales: breathes out

hibernation: an inactive or sleeping state

migrating: moving from one region to another

weaned: when a baby animal stops drinking the mother's milk

INDEX

Arctic 8, 10, 14, 18
Arctic Ocean 4
babies 20
birds 12
blind 20
camouflage 6
carnivores 6
claws 7
coat 6, 14
cubs 20, 23
den 20, 23
dormant 20
ears 6, 7

eggs 12
exhales 15
freeze 10
fur 6, 20
global warming 18
hibernation 20
hunt 4, 14, 16-17, 18-19
ice 4, 7, 8, 10, 11, 15, 16, 18, 23
ice floes 8
litter 20
migrating 11
nose 7
oil spills 19
paws 7

pollution 19
prey 6, 14
rodents 12
scientists 18
seals 7, 11, 12, 14-15, 16, 18, 23
shellfish 12
shore 18
snow 4, 7, 14, 20
swimmers 4
temperatures 4, 18
walruses 17
water 4, 8
weaned 23
whales 17